Ways of knowing

God's existence
and his will

John C Edwards SJ

Gracewing

Originally published in 1997 by Family Publications

This edition 2012

Gracewing
2 Southern Avenue
Leominster
Herefordshire HR6 0QF

www.gracewing.co.uk

ISBN 978 0 85244 800 7

Contents

Foreword

How shall I find out God's will for me? Does God exist anyway, and how can I find out about his existence and nature? These two questions have been of profound and perennial interest since the human race began; people have stumbled along the path of discovery, in ancient Greece, Israel and elsewhere. They are of profound significance and cannot afford to be side-stepped.

In his new book Father John Edwards offers us explorations and answers to these ancient questions. God in his three persons has not left us without vital clues in our search for answers to the first question. In the Trinity God offers us the power to discover his will, through his control of circumstance, through his Word in revelation and through the discernment that comes to us through the grace of the Holy Spirit. About ways of acting there can be no doubt. The Ten Commandments leave us quite clear directives; but beyond that we do need to discern God's will and here we are helped by the rules of discernment of spirit as they are offered to us in the *Spiritual Exercises* of St Ignatius Loyola.

In Part 2 Father Edwards presents the classical arguments for the existence of God, above all based on contingency; and shows in addition the ultimate inadequacy of a determinist vision of the universe.

It is good to have these important truths put before us in a clear and uncluttered way and I welcome Father Edwards' approach warmly.

†Mario Conti, Bishop of Aberdeen

Dedicated to my niece Charlotte

by the same author:
Ways of Praying
Ways of Forgiveness
Ways of Knowing
A New and Special Way

Fr John Edwards was born in Sussex and was educated at Ampleforth and the Royal Naval College, Dartmouth. He went to sea in 1947 and served in the Korean war, leaving the Navy in 1953 to seek his vocation with the Society of Jesus. He was ordained priest in 1964 and continued his studies in Rome. Since 1968 he has served in parishes and more recently in retreat work and parish missions which have taken him several times to the USA, and to Albania, Iceland, Mauritius, New Zealand and various countries in Africa

Preface

For the believer there is nothing more important than to
do God's will. It is for this we are created and this is
our fulfilment. Nothing else could make us happy. And
of course God's will, at one level, is the one thing that
we are bound to be getting; for nothing can happen that
is not willed directly, or at least permitted, by God.

From this it should follow that happiness is always
ours . . . Does one want anything other than what God
wants? No. And one has what God wants? Yes. So
is there anything lacking, anything for which God is not
to be praised and thanked? Are we not all in the
condition the advertisers speak of – "the man who has
everything"?

Although for some reason this argument breaks
down in practice, it is a fact that none of us could wish,
however often we fail to do it, anything that is not
God's will. But this book is not about the doing of
God's will: that sort of thing needs to be written by a
saint. Rather it is about the theory of *finding* God's
will. This of course involves the process known as
"discernment of spirits". I am writing about the theory,
drawing mainly on St Ignatius. About the charismatic
gift of discernment, which certainly exists and which I
have seen in operation by others, I know nothing.

The first part of the book, *Ways of knowing God's
Will*, is precisely about that. It is meant for those who
want a serious relationship with God: in my mind have
been all those who are devoted to God's will wherever

and however he has called them, those who think that God may be calling them to something very different, and all concerned Religious. It will be obvious from the text that at different times I address different sorts of people.

The second part is very different, and its relevance may seem remote. It is written for Christian young people. I envisage some of my readers as being teenagers who are perplexed enough to be worried by the names Stephen Hawking and Richard Dawkins but patient enough to read the text and to try to think it out, preferably with the guidance of a Christian teacher. Reading it may be hard work, although the text is over-simple, a bare minimum. But it does seem that young Christians are deprived of basic tools of thought, and even vocabulary, for serious thought about theological and philosophical matters. For thinking straight about God, and therefore ultimately for discernment of spirits, this needs correction

Where the first part is all about God and response to him, the second part prescinds from him more or less, except when it is a question of "proving" his existence. And the name of Christ is not mentioned. This of course is because what is involved is the use of reason alone, without advertence to revelation.

I am deeply indebted to Sister Monica Gribbin RHSM, Fathers Anthony Meredith SJ and Michael Barber SJ for their guidance and comments. I have also been encouraged by the kind comments of Sister Briege McKenna OSC and Father Graham Leonard.

For Bishop Conti's generous gift of his precious time and his gracious foreword, I am deeply grateful.

John Edwards SJ
London, September 1997

Part I

Ways of knowing
God's will

One:

God's will and the Love of God: the "areas"

1. To love God is to do his will

The best practical definition of love is that it is *to want, and to try to do, always, what is the best for the other person.* To want, notice; not to feel. To *intend*, not to emote. Surely there is place for feeling in love, and it would be odd to want and to try to do something perhaps heroically demanding for someone, without any bonding emotion at all. But feelings are not the essence.

If love were simply a matter of feeling, then no one could promise it – for we cannot promise to feel. We can only promise what is in our control. So too no one could ever get married, for in marriage you promise to love; you can't promise to feel, you can only promise what is possible. Notice too that if love is a matter primarily of intending, of willing, then duty, which so often has a cold and reluctant feel to it, can in fact sometimes be another name for love. See too that our Lord orders us to love our enemies, which he could not do if to love them demanded that we should be feeling fond of them.

What then is the love of God? It is, obviously, *to want, and to try to do, always, what is the best for God.* And what is the "best for God"? Plainly, what he wants, his will. If that is so, to love God – the aim of life, the joy of all the saints, the purpose of our existence, the fulfilment of all our desires for all eternity – simply consists in doing what God wants.

2. All I ever need to know and to do is God's will

If then I want to be successful in life, in the next life as well as this one, all I ever have to do is the will of God. Of course I should do it *totally*, not grudgingly. It is not enough to say "Well, if God wants this, then I suppose I'd better submit". That might be all I could be capable of, but truly to want the will of the beloved, which is what we have defined love to be, will involve my embracing with alacrity and with all the enthusiasm I can muster what he has chosen for me. Easier said, of course, than done.

If to love God is what I am for, and to do his will is the way to love, then life consists simply in finding the will of God and doing it. There is nothing worth doing, ever, except knowing what God wants and trying to do it as generously as one can. Any believer can see that, even the greatest sinner. Of course, while the principle is clear, the doing of it demands heroism.

This *doing* of the will of God is the work of sanctity. And after the example and teaching of good Christian parents, the best way of learning would be seeing how very holy and generous people live their lives, and trying to emulate them. The *finding* of the will of God, provided of course I do really want to know, need not be so difficult or so painful. And there is a fair body of teaching about it. Of course for the finer points in this learning and finding, holiness is needed. Even so, one would have to be an earnest and sensitive lover to detect the subtler indications of what the beloved would really like. But much of the "theory" can be expounded by any ordinary sinner. This book is, in fact, just such an exposition.

3. Three masters

The grounds of the theory do however, as you would expect, come from great lovers of God: from saints or teachers of saints. The doctrine that follows is taken, almost in its entirety, from St Ignatius of Loyola (*Spiritual Exercises* and *Letter on obedience*), Fr Louis Lallement SJ (*Spiritual Teaching*) and Fr Jean-Pierre de Caussade SJ (*Abandonment to Divine Providence*). Except possibly for the consideration of the "areas" of God's will which immediately follows, and the token theology, probably everything in Part 1 is drawn from these three giants.

4. God's will comes in three "areas", each "appropriated" to the persons of the Blessed Trinity: Circumstances, Obedience, Discernment

In considering his will, it helps first to consider God himself. God is One; his nature is One. His nature is *what* he is: what, so to speak, he "works" with. Just as you and I "work" and live by our human nature, and *what* we are is our manhood or womanhood or our profession. *Who* God is, is denoted by the word "person". If someone asks who you are, the answer is your name. Who is God? God is three persons: Father, Son, Holy Spirit. *What* the Father is, is God; *what* the Son, is God and Man; *what* the Spirit, is God. Different persons, all with the same nature. "Outside" the life of the Blessed Trinity itself all the works of God are done with the use of his one nature.

This is not the place to discuss how the Church

worked its way through to a coherent way of thinking about God. This is not a book of theology. But it must be emphasised that any Christian who is capable of reading this far and has found the last paragraph surprising, surely has a clear duty to get hold of a book such as Frank Sheed's *Theology and Sanity* and getting the ideas clear.

It is customary however, and it helps, and it is reasonable, and it is in conformity with Scripture, to see that some particular works that God does are more "appropriate", as it were, to one or other person. Thus it is instinctive to associate the work of creation to God the Father; the work of redemption to God the Son. It evidently seemed "appropriate" also to God himself that it should be the Word, the Wisdom of God, that should take human flesh and enter this bent and lunatic world to put it right. The work of healing and sanctifying is appropriate to God the Holy Spirit. This procedure is in fact known as "appropriation".

There is a sense in which one can say that the three persons of the Blessed Trinity, while having only one will "external" to themselves, have certain areas of it which can be *appropriated* to each one. What follows is a consideration of *circumstances* being appropriated to God the Father, looked on as creator and conserver; of his expressed will, the area of *obedience* being appropriated to the word, wisdom of God – the Son; of his good advice and *counsel* being appropriated to the Spirit.

Two:

God the Father – Circumstances

1. Examples

To God the Father, creator and conserver, can be appropriated the area of *Circumstances*. The disposition of every atom and molecule and pulse of energy in the universe, the content of every moment of time – all this is God's will. One might object: these cancer cells and the agony they cause, are you saying that God, our dear and loving Father, wills these? Well, yes. If that is too painful to admit, at least one must say that he permits them. If he did not will them, permit them, then one would have to say that here was part of his creation, namely these cancer cells, that had escaped from his power and providence: in short, that God was incompetent.

Suppose the cancer cells were there through the sufferer's own stupid or sinful action, or suppose the "circumstances" we consider are the wounding of a victim by another's sin? Yet still we must say that the result in the victim's body is willed or, if you insist, permitted. God does not will the sin in the assailant, but the ordinary workings of nature consequent on the evil action are assuredly part of his providence.

Though God wills or allows the circumstances of the present moment, he may well want me to alter the circumstances so that the next moment may be different. I need to answer the doorbell. I'm not praying just now; but I should be. Although God allows that my leg should be broken, it is also his will that I get it mended. It is God's will my hands should be dirty just now; it is also his will that I should wash them. That said, it must be emphasised that at this split second of time there can be no possible doubt about what God has willed or allowed: it is dictated to me by the circumstances of the present moment.

2. The "Sacrament of the present moment"
So loving God is easy?

God's will in this area is perfectly clear. I mean, I can be in no doubt at all what the air temperature in this room should be, according to God's will, at this moment: he's got it the way he wants it. At least, if he hasn't got it the way he wants it, something has gone very wrong with his omnipotence and his providence. Of course he might want me to change the air temperature by shutting the window. But this is a different department or area of God's will, the area of "good advice" or counsel, which will be treated below. And if I have broken my leg there can be no doubt that it has happened, and that an all-powerful and all-loving God has permitted it when he could have stopped it. Also, he presumably wants me to get the leg mended; but that again is obedience in a different area of God's will.

So I know exactly how old and how fit God wants me to be at this time: I've got his will. Obviously I could do with losing a bit of weight – that also is God's will, I suppose - but that too is in a different area. The point is, the circumstances at this moment of time are exactly as God has willed (or allowed). Therefore, I can be completely at peace about my age and health, and indeed all other circumstances of my life. I should praise and thank, never grumble; for God, who can never will evil to me, can only have apportioned these circumstances to me as capable of leading to his greater glory and my own fulfilment. I may have to do something to change these circumstances, but at this moment of time I know exactly what God wants.

Since to do God's will is to love him, then as Fr de Caussade would say, there can be nothing easier, more available at every moment of time, than to love him; for this consists simply in embracing the will of God at every moment. He will say that the abyss of the love of God, bigger than all our desires, has as its entrance a very narrow cleft into which one must dive: this cleft is the present moment. He calls it a Sacrament, the present moment; for a Sacrament is an outward sign of an inward grace or union with God; and every moment offers an opportunity for this, since every moment brings the duty of doing the will of God. And this is love, and love means union. He says that highest sanctity consists in the pursuit of God through *what so effectively disguises him* – namely the present moment.

The theory is easy enough to see. But of course the practice is difficult. The impact of every moment on me brings a duty not just of acceptance, but of reacting – and usually to a DUTY. If one were ever tempted to think sanctity were easy, it is enough to remember that for most people the raw material of their love of God is their love – that is, in practice, their service – of others. This book is a manual on finding God's will, not on charity or the love of God. But it must be pointed out that my success in loving God, the measure of my holiness and of my true success in life, is likely to be my performance in obeying the second great commandment: Love your neighbour as yourself. God is telling me to be as concerned about, as sensitive to, as thoughtful for *others* as I am about myself. What I do, or fail to do, for others towards whom this present moment brings a duty, is a principal criterion of my love of God.

3. Since God is all good and all powerful, every circumstance is Gift

Since God is a dear and loving Father and is all-powerful, his will *must* be capable of redounding to his glory and to my fulfilment. Sometimes it is not difficult to accept this, because his will may be very pleasant. There are innumerable joys to be experienced which may be God's will for us. In fact the keynote of Christian life, for reasons which will be apparent later, is ordinarily nothing other than joy: in this life as well as in the next.

Most people's lives are studded with moments of experience of joy and beauty. Maybe not earth-shattering moments, but genuine joys and beauties nonetheless. We should probably train ourselves to notice these more, and not to be, as some are, chronically obsessed with their opposites, pains and ugliness.

But God knows there are enough of these. They too are gifts: nasty gifts, but still coming from God's hands. God's expressed will can often be quite hideous and absolutely appalling, as even a few moments watching an average TV news bulletin, or nature programme, can often prove. To handle this we have to be obsessed with the cross, and skilled in the art of cross-carrying.

Consider. The worst thing that ever happened was Calvary; yet it produced the greatest good. If God can

18

manage to bring success out of the worst horror, he is perfectly capable of doing the same thing out of lesser evils. As has been said before, a good and all-powerful God could not allow anything to happen which was not capable of redounding to his Glory – which has to be the purpose of creation – and consequently to our good.

The Irish had a beautiful saying to help them through the myriad disasters of their history: "Blessed be the Holy Will of God". And our Pentecostal brethren would be insistent, rightly, that "God is to be *praised and thanked* for EVERYTHING". For *everything*? Well, yes: unless, that is, that he is incompetent or malicious . . . Is God good or isn't he? Is he omnipotent or not?

If in fact he does know what he is doing, these circumstances of the present moment are an outward sign of an invisible union-gift: a sort of sacrament in fact, as de Caussade says. The spiritual skill known as "offering it up" is the way of turning our small crosses to good account. If we are in a state of grace, Christ lives in us. What we suffer, or do, is suffered and done in some sense "by" him: when we join our sufferings to his we are doing what St Paul says: "I help to pay off the debt which the afflictions of Christ still leave to be paid, for the sake of his body, the Church" (*Col* 1:24).

4. His will is clear

His will in this area is not only gift, it is also absolutely clear. To repeat: there can be no doubt at all if one is lying at the bottom of the stairs with a broken leg. Or if one has had a stroke. Or if the biopsy has said cancer. Or if this terrorist bomb has gone off. In all the vast territory of life that is comprised in the situation as it is, I can have no doubt at all what God has dictated. And no doubt at all of how I am to love him, for loving God simply consists in doing, and embracing his will.

Remember too that the ability I have to love him, the opening to me of the highest sanctity (which simply consists in doing his will), is available to me at every moment, and is entirely possible. If it were not possible, it could not, of course, be his will.

There is no moment when God's will, dictated through circumstances, is not open to me. Imagine one was damned ("Depart from me you cursed . . . !") and, if you wish, tumbling into the abyss: if one were able to say "Lord, this is the ultimate and utter disaster; but it is your will. Therefore I praise and thank you and embrace your will . . .", isn't it plain that hell would evaporate for one at that very instant? The doing of his will is always possible, and the doing of it always brings union with him.

How practical and possible the doctrine of the sacrament of the present moment makes the love and service of God seem. All I ever have to do is to do what he wants at this moment, carry the cross of this moment. So much of life for the Christian does not consist in doing anything different from the unbeliever: doing things with a different motive, yes; but highest sanctity for the Christian, as rational life for the unbeliever, may involve no more than shopping in a supermarket or going to bed. "What so *effectively* disguises Him", says Fr de Caussade.

5. The problem of evil

"If God were all-powerful he *could* prevent all suffering and evil. If he were all good he *would* prevent it. But suffering and evil exist. Therefore God is either *not* all-powerful or *not* all good. Therefore God (in Christian terms) does not exist". This is the classic statement of the "problem of evil". Probably most of the readers of these pages will have answered this to their satisfaction, but in case anyone has been startled by any of the statements made in preceding paragraphs, a few words might be appropriate.

Christians say that God could have prevented all suffering and evil, but did not. This, not because he is bad, but because he is good. Being good he gives good gifts to his creation. One of these gifts is that humans will live forever, another is that he gives them power to love. To love, not just to feel affection (animals can do that), but - our definition in the first words of the text - to "want, and to try to do, whatever is best for the other person, or people".

For this he has to give freedom. You cannot be said to choose if you cannot *help* deciding as you do. But this gift is a dangerous one. It is possible to choose badly, wrongly, selfishly. Most of the sufferings people endure in this life have been the result of bad, wrong, selfish choices: think of all the results through the ages of war, vice, slavery, cruelty, wrong ambition. God cannot really be blamed: he gave a good gift, we misused it.

But if we live for ever, the damage done to our "system of choice", to ourselves, could be permanent and could last for ever . . . this would be hell. It could be that we could choose so wrongly that we could mutilate ourselves permanently, eradicate from ourselves the equipment we need (supernatural grace, the life of the soul). This would result in us being fixed in eternal agony in our proximity to God.

Looked at in this way it is reasonable to think of hell

not so much as a result of a judgement made by God (*Mt* 25), as a ratification by God of a judgement we have made on ourselves ("Very well, not my will but *thine* be done"). And there is nothing God can do about it. Cannot he stop it hurting? Only if he annihilates us, if he stops us existing. Cannot he force us to love him, force us to change our minds? Only if he takes away our free will. But for neither case can there be a "change of mind" in God.

This line of thinking is traditional and orthodox. But it does not help explain suffering which is not dependent on the wrong choice of men. So what of "physical" evil, including the sufferings of animals – where men are not the cause of it. What follows is also traditional thought, but does not have the same degree of probability.

If Satan were the guardian angel, a spirit of vast power and intelligence and with some sort of stewardship over God's creation, appointed for this world – or this universe – some light is possible. Satan averts himself from God the same way that we do, through wrong choice. God does not annihilate him; he still has immense power and some sort of control. But he is now fixed in hatred of God and of everything that speaks to him of God: of every atom and molecule, all of which exist through God's love and power; still more of every living organism, especially of animals; still more of mankind, made in God's image. Now Satan cannot create, but he could surely *distort* and damage and deface God's creation, and at a very deep and intimate level.

This does not "answer" the dark mystery of evil. One is entitled to ask (what can never be answered) "why did God create an angel knowing that . . . etc".

But it throws some light. The only real answer, the practical answer, is of course the cross. About which some words later.

6. Gifts of grace – Baptism and its effects

We should never be oblivious to the natural good things that God gives. But the gifts of grace outweigh them. God is present "in" all things, including us, as part of the natural order of things. But to one "in a state of grace" as the technical term has it, the presence is in a different category. To be in a state of grace means to have in one, as a principle of action, the very life of Christ himself; it is to have in an extraordinary way the gift, created, of a share in the life of God; it is to have a union with God of unimaginable intimacy, and one utterly undeserved.

This gift would normally come in baptism. Part of the present-moment joy could be to know that with this life one will have the equipment one needs to enjoy God for all eternity. Then too, though the word is distasteful the concept is inevitable, there is the question of "merit". If God the Father sees his Son living and working in me, of course he cannot not respond. And for every action of ours that is not sinful there is bound to be reward.

7. Reconciliation and its effects

We would do well to think more about the sacraments, and not just baptism, as having a *present* effect in our lives. Every sacrament has a long-term effect as well as a short term one. Take the sacrament of reconciliation. Short term of course the effect is complete forgiveness, and complete certainty about it. Providing I want to try to live the way our Lord wants, the way the Church asks, then the sacrament brings judgement and forgiveness. It is not the priest but God who is the judge, as he is also jury. The verdict he gives is "NOT GUILTY"; as judge he says "CASE DISMISSED". And forgiveness by God means that Jesus intervenes in my life, at every bad moment of the past, to cover each bad moment with his precious blood. The whole of my life becomes a complete success story; and the worse it was, the more beautiful it is now. That is not because I have done anything to merit this; it is because Jesus has intervened at great cost, and repeatedly, to do this unimaginably generous work.

When God has judged, Satan has no appeal against the verdict. From this moment back to the beginning of my life, God will never judge again. That means that though I may weep for my sins, the tears must be of joy and gratitude and the sweetest sorrow: I am never allowed to agonize about the past. Nor am I allowed to be in guilt towards the dead whom I may have failed: when God forgives, all those who are dead, and who (if they see at all) see things as God sees them, see not my offence but only that Jesus has done something so costly and so beautiful for me.

But there is a long-term effect too. The Church prays through the priest after the conferring of Absolution: "May the Passion of our Lord Jesus Christ, the merits of the Blessed Virgin Mary, and of all the Saints, whatever good you do, and whatever evil you suffer, gain for you the forgiveness of sin, increase of grace and the reward of eternal life". The interesting words are *whatever evil you suffer*. This includes spiritual evils: temptations, weaknesses – perhaps our own fault – which could have damned us. Now, by God's extraordinary chemistry, these very horrors are going to bring us closer to him! Of course we are not allowed to sin . . . but the weaknesses that are capable of no more than sin are now perhaps the best and most useful gift we have.

Therefore if one is considering the "present moment", one would be foolish not to consider this wonderful sacrament which not only has the power to acquit me of all guilt and to render my life a triumph in God's sight, but which dashes Satan's preferred weapons from his hands and uses them against him. "O happy fault, O truly necessary sin of Adam which merited so great a redemption". So also of each one of us, when the offences have been brought to the Body of Christ in the sacrament and received his saving touch. The sacrament can restore the life of Christ to me and enrich me in the very point of my emptiness. And of course if *that* is the situation in me at this moment there isn't really much else that is a threat.

8. Anointing of the sick and its effects

There is an immediate effect too in the Sacrament of Anointing: the forgiveness of sin, and if God wishes, healing. But there is a long-term effect too, as there is with Reconciliation and indeed with all the sacraments. In this one, Christ has touched the sufferer, and touched the sickness. That is why one should expect healing. But if he does not heal, God has still touched. So what will happen to this cancer, say, or these hardened arteries or these gasping lungs? The illness is going to go on, the final terminal illness is going to kill the person . . . *but the sick organ, the damaged tissues, have been touched*

25

by Christ. That means that they are in some sense "holy" in spite of all their horror, because, touched by Christ *they are going to make the person holy*. As they proceed, doing their dirty work and squeezing the physical life out of the sufferer, they are conferring Christ's life on the sufferer. The sick man knows he has now, in every circumstance however painful, humiliating, frightening, exactly what he needs – calculated by God! – to bring him from this point straight into his Father's arms.

9. Marriage and its effects – and the other sacraments

The married couple have too at each moment a special gift. As in the other sacraments what happened was that through the Church Jesus *touched* them. Now a touch from Jesus effects something. In marriage, the bodies of the man and the woman were touched, with the result that every loving contact, every action involving love, is not only going to be humanly desirable, useful, warm, supportive, helpful – whatever it is, from making love, to doing the washing-up, to mowing the lawn, to going out to work – but it is *going to make the other person holy*. The sacrament means that every good action to do with the marriage is above all else going to work as an effective prayer for the other.

As to the other sacraments, the same principle holds. The "sacramental grace", known in some of them as the "character" or seal, has a lasting effect. Very relevant to what comes later, *Confirmation* will among other things entitle one to expect some facility in *discernment*, always assuming I live in such a way as to let the power be operative. The *Eucharist* among so much else is the *pledge of eternal glory*, setting up what is really something more than a nuptial bond between me and Jesus. *Priesthood*, enabling Jesus to do his own priestly work with infallible effect through this sinful man, among all else would cement a union between the two in the very exercise of the ministry.

Three:

The Word – Law, Obedience

1. God speaks

To God the Son, the word and the wisdom of the Father, is appropriated all the area of God's expressed Will, what one may call the area of *Obedience*. The Word himself it is who speaks and proclaims his commandments. One facet of this proclamation is our human nature. Some things we see lead us to our natural fulfilment, some do not. It is a "law" of human nature, a "natural law", that I flourish on potatoes and wither away on strychnine. This is a law mankind found out by trial and error. But there are other "natural laws", which ought to be discoverable by man but sometimes are not, which God has to reveal. One of these is that sex in marriage leads to life, outside of marriage it leads to a "death" of one sort or another.

In this latter case the Christian will see that the life/dying might be eternal, whereas the potatoes/strychnine life is merely temporal. It looks as if God took the trouble to tell us directly a good deal about the ways of eternal life-enhancement and eternal life-denial, as if these things were too important to be left to our own powers of deduction from the facts of our nature.

God in fact did more. When he wedded himself to our human nature, by what we Christians call the Incarnation, he also built human beings in an extraordinary way into himself: he had a physical body, he now incorporates human beings into a mystical body through which he continues to work. For practical purposes we can equate this mystical body with the Church. It continues the work Jesus did on earth in his physical body: it makes his saving action present, it makes holy, it can heal. And it teaches and it legislates. Acceptance of the teaching of the Church is acceptance of Jesus' teaching, and obedience to the Church's laws is obedience to the will of God.

The reader who is not a Catholic must make the necessary adaptations here. It may be that there seem to be no clear certainties laid down by God, and nothing to go by except "conscience" and, as regards revelation, what seems reasonable to one's own intelligence. That position would throw doubt on much of what appears here. The Catholic position is very different.

2. Conscience

This is ALWAYS to be obeyed. There is never an occasion when a man should not follow his conscience, any more than a man should not see what is visible. But to say "you must follow your conscience" is really no more helpful than to say "you must see what you see". There isn't anything else *to* see. Conscience is an act of judging. To be told to follow it is to be told to judge as you judge.

The subtlety is in judging rightly. And just as a man who has lost his spectacles, and in thick fog runs across a double line of traffic, can judge wrongly, and disastrously, so can erroneous and disastrous judgements be made – perhaps in the best of faith – in matters of right and wrong. Our judgements, as we all know, can be wrong. To be told by God the facts of the situation, to be told which way leads to life, which way gives him glory, which way leads to fulfilment, is to have a short-cut certainty as to how to judge rightly, an exhilarating privilege and a glorious entry into freedom. Just as the discovery of the aerofoil section led to the freedom to fly, so the revelation by God of, say, the right use of sex, is for us a liberation from slavery into a freedom we would hardly have guessed at for ourselves.

To attempt to coerce anyone else's conscience is an attempt to violate their most sacred human gift, their power to judge and to decide. In fact of course it can't be done. One could only force people to act *against* their conscience.

Conscience of course has to be trained, for it is an act of the practical judgement about whether, here and now, this action is good or bad and to be done or not. And judgement needs to be trained.

3. Obedience to whom?

Obedience to God's Law is the key to successful human living; break the Law, and I break myself. But the Church's law is man-made, and if it ever conflicted with what God wanted, it would in principle be correct to disregard it for the sake of the higher Law. But in practice, since the Church has authority from Christ not just to teach (which it can do infallibly) but also to legislate – something that is necessary for any organisation made up of human beings, even though that organisation be the mystical body of Christ – normally to obey the Church is to obey Christ.

Notice that obedience need not be a harsh word. It need not be a soldier's word, nor a child's, nor a slave's. Contrary to what many feel it is not an insult to be asked to obey. Dancers are obedient to the music of the dance: a lover is obedient to the desire and the embrace of the beloved.

4. There is usually little about what God wants

I do not have to wonder whether it is alright for me to commit adultery: God has (literally) spelled it out for me in a book: I can't. Nor need I weigh up whether, being in good health and close to a church, I might miss Mass next Sunday. Both these laws are clear enough: the former a law of God, the latter a law of the Church. And human lawgivers, justly appointed, have their authority from God when their laws are just. All this is the area of *Obedience*, and it is normally clear enough. I do not usually have to puzzle whether our Lord might want me to cheat on my taxes; or, if I am a religious, to pull a fast one on my superior. In all these cases our Lord has told me, explicitly enough, that in each case the answer is "no".

When it is a case of any human law, there could never be a question of being bound to something immoral. But there is a further point that is relevant in Church law. One must always assume that the lawgiver is not a fool, or does not intend the good of the subject. Therefore when I can be clear that the lawgiver would not intend me to be bound by his regulation, taking into account the circumstances, I can feel free to disregard the obligation. This is called the use of *equity*, or *epikeia*. For instance, it is against the law to drive on the wrong side of the road: but nobody wants to charge the driver of a fire-engine for doing so in an emergency. You cannot really say there is disobedience; the *mind* of the lawgiver is being followed at the expense of the letter of his law.

5. Religious obedience

Here there is a special clarity about obedience. The vow basically binds the subject to our Lord in such a way that every act done in obedience to the "superior", who has been appointed as such by the human mechanisms of what is in truth the bride and very body of Christ – namely the Church – will result in an act of worship. The actions will not just be good, and therefore spiritually meritorious and enriching the whole Church as do all good actions, but over and above that they are enacted so to speak in the very sanctuary of God: the "scene of your approach now" is that spoken of in *Hebrews* 12:22-25.

The basic fundamental insight, however exegetes may disapprove, is the fact that "he who hears you hears me" (*Lk* 10:16). The basic structure of obedience for the religious is the constitutions which are the expression of the will of Jesus for me now; the way his advice in the Sermon on the Mount is concretized today. It is an effect of the incarnation that God's will is made present to me through the fallible will and intelligence of a human being. More about this later. Of course, as has been said, there is no question of "obedience" to a command which is sinful. Now many of my readers are likely to be Religious, with a vow of obedience. They are unlikely to need reassurance that, while the highest superior (as Canon law says) is the Pope, still obedience to the just directives of lower superiors is also obedience to our Lord himself.

It is worth remembering that the Religious vows

obedience, not efficiency. The sinful command (were it to occur) could never be "obeyed"; the inefficient command causes some complexity, to be dealt with briefly later. But in practice all the life of the Religious, in outline, should be directed by obedience – through men directly to Jesus Christ.

To repeat: it is the singular privilege of the Religious to have every act of every day pleasing to God through the virtue of the vow. God receives glory from each simple human action, not just because it is the act of a Christian in a state of grace (and therefore seen by God as in some sense as "done" by his Son, and therefore meritorious), but because for the person with vows it becomes a direct act of direct worship of God.

6. The freedom and glory of obedience

Obedience brings me the will of God. Therefore to obey, totally and generously, is to love God. When the family has to do the washing-up, and granted that God wants nothing else at that moment, then that is the holiest thing I can be doing. Also, since what I want is to love God, and that is what my happiness consists in, and since to do God's will is to love God, then to do the washing-up is my greatest happiness . . . And incidentally the greatest exercise of my freedom, because a man is totally free when he is able to do exactly what he wants to do, and in this case what he wants to do is God's will . . . Let us admit that such joys can be very "spiritual" indeed, and are not normally experienced other than in faith; but the relationship of love/obedience, freedom, happiness is clear enough.

All this may sound theoretical, but in fact it is not as outrageous as it may seem, even to a man who would lay no claims to great holiness. After all, if I know that this activity is truly what God wants of me, is there anything else on earth in my deepest heart (suffocate it though I may try) that I would rather do? Is there anything else on earth which I can seriously think is going to give me a moment's true joy? I may be a fool and a villain and skimp God's will, through laziness or melancholy or selfishness, but I know even before and even as I avoid the will of God that I am stepping into some level of misery.

7. Representation

There is one subtlety about obedience which is sometimes not appreciated, and which certainly used to be ignored. It is the matter of "representation". I speak first for Religious, but it affects all Christians, for all are under the law of God and of the Church.

It has to be assumed that the superior is not an imbecile, and is not so blind with self-conceit that he or she thinks they know the answer to everything. It is possible for the superior to be wrong. (In the olden days, it sometimes seemed very difficult for some of them to admit this). Now, charged as they are by God with the heavy responsibility of keeping their community happy and united, and with probably massive responsibilities in the public arena, one would hope that they would be glad to accept help in the discharge of their duties. Since the Holy Spirit blows in various quarters, it is not impossible that he might tell something to one of the "subjects" that he does not tell the superior. The subject might have knowledge that the superior does not have.

If this is the case, it would obviously be a sin against

charity, as well as a sin against obedience, if the subject did not tell the superior. The attitude of the latter should be "Oh, thanks so much for telling me". *Should be.* Old-timers only need to look back to their noviceship to think of the occasions when one would never have dared, as one valued one's vocation, ever to risk saying anything that would have been interpreted as "criticism of the superior".

It is indeed possible to think that what happened so commonly in the 1960s in religious life, namely the revolutionary change in the attitude to obedience and to so much of the traditional way to God, would not have occurred if through generations previously there had not been what was in fact a betrayal of obedience, through the atrophy of the practice of representation.

Representation is not something that affects Religious only. The principle holds for all Christians. If I think the catechetical text-book that my children have to use has teaching contrary to the Church's; if my parish priest is certainly contravening the liturgical regulations; if the retreat house staff concelebrate Mass with non-Catholic clergy, then I have a duty in charity and in obedience to tell the appropriate authority. In charity: it shouldn't be done in a rage. It should be done after prayer, and quite likely after consulting someone prudent and faithful and knowledgeable. Never, never, never is it done anonymously. And there is no need to do it if there is moral certainty that it will do no good. It has got to be about something serious.

If it is done, and again if the matter is serious there is a duty not just in charity but even in obedience to represent, the best way might normally be to approach, with courtesy and gentleness and good humour, the person responsible. If this produces no result, then the next step would be, always assuming that the matter is worth all this upheaval, to go to a higher superior – stating, if one can, the reasons for the previous refusal.

When the answer comes back, and it probably will for the religious: "Well, thanks for telling me: but I think we'll do it my way". Then of course one could take it to a higher superior, if it is worth it. If one were to do so, one would probably get an answer "I think the person on the spot probably is the best judge; best go along with it".

The non-religious is usually dismissed as a trouble-maker. "I think you must be mistaken and have misheard what was said; no one else on the retreat made any complaint". Then what? Well, always assuming the matter is serious, the best and bravest thing to do would be to write to the Bishop, with copies to the perpetrator of the abuse and to the Apostolic Delegate. Tell the story; and make a point of getting a reply to these questions. Assuming I am right in my facts, is what I tell you a serious matter? Did I do right to tell you?

8. The three levels of obedience; the high point

We are involved in one aspect of what Ignatius sees as the very perfection of obedience. He speaks of three degrees of obedience. The first is that of *execution,* when I do what I've been told. He thinks little of that: after all, a performing seal will do what it's told; one can do what one is told while seething with resentment and a sense of injustice. For St Ignatius just to do what one is told does not count as obedience. No, for it to be *spiritual* obedience one must embrace the order with the *Will,* one must *love* what one has been commanded. But suppose one can't: suppose whatever construction one puts on it, it still looks stupid or unfair or likely to cause trouble?

Then, says St Ignatius, one proceeds to the highest degree of obedience, that of the *Understanding*. I work away to try to embrace with my understanding what authority is saying. I try to see it the way the superior sees it. If I succeed, then I have obedience "of the understanding". Suppose however it still looks stupid, no matter how I try to understand it? So then, I share my understanding of the affair with the superior: I "represent". If I do, I am again obeying with my understanding and doing something the saint praised. Representation, described above, is part of the highest level of obedience. It might of course be sinful if I did not do it. What failure of love there would be, let alone failure of obedience, if I allowed the superior to damage the work of God because he lacked the information I knowingly withheld from him.

What if the superior does not accept my understanding of the matter? Then comes the third level of obedience of the understanding. I now know what God wants. It still looks pretty disastrous, but I can have no doubt that this is the course of action he wants. (Again, there is no question of obeying if I were ordered to do something unjust or sinful). My job now is still to obey with the will. To do this I have attempted to align my understanding with that of the superior; I've failed; I have tried to share my understanding through representation; I've failed. Now comes a third process in obedience of the understanding, which I adopt in order finally to embrace with the intellect what the superior (and God) want – so that my will, my love, can be engaged.

What I do is to open my eyes wide to all the *motives* for going along with it. The motives, not the facts. I know the facts very well; they look appalling; I've probably represented them. It is the *motive* now that I need if I am to weld my understanding to what I now know is God's "understanding", so that my will may be joined to God's, so that I may obey with the will, so that I may love what is commanded.

One could call this level of obedience of the understanding therefore "open-eyed" obedience, because now one knows one must do the thing, one needs all the helpful motives one can get. Any innocent motive will do. "Well, he's not a bad old stick; I don't want to make him unhappy". "It'll please some of the others, anyway". "It's not all that important, I suppose". "It's time I had a dirty job, and it'll let someone else off". And, of course, the serious positive motive: "Father, not my will but thine be done: now, Lord, at last I begin to imitate you".

Or, since the process would involve also shutting one's eyes to motives for *not* doing the thing, one could as well call it "shut-eyed" obedience. Blind obedience, in fact. And this is what it has been traditionally called, this third leg of obedience of the understanding. Notice the blindness is to the motives, not the facts. It is not military obedience; not the obedience of the soldier told to shoot prisoners. It is an act helping me to do what I know now with certainty is God's will. It is not mysterious; we do it, or at least many of us do, every time we get out of bed. There are many apparently good motives for staying in. Better not think of them; better just do it. Our Lord, of course, practised blind obedience in the Garden of Gethsemane. Presumably it is a process adopted by every martyr that there has ever been. Obviously, blind obedience might be the bravest and most costly and holiest thing God asks.

9. Summary

To sum up:

Obedience

1. of Execution (need not be true obedience at all)
2. of the Will, when I love and embrace what I must do
3. of the Understanding, to help me obey with the will:
   - I can bring myself to accept with my understanding that what I'm being asked to do is the best
   - I can't incline my understanding like that, so I share my understanding with the superior – I represent
   - if this fails, or if it isn't serious enough to warrant representation, then I shut my eyes to all the motives that would hinder my doing of what I now know is God's Will – "blind" obedience.

Four:

The Holy Spirit:
Counsel, God's good advice

To the Holy Spirit the third area of *Discernment* is attributed. This is the area of his good advice, his counsel. Unlike the other two areas it may be very unclear what God is advising. I know I ought to pray; but how much? When? In what manner? Where? I know I ought to fast; but how much? When? What effect might there be on the family? I know I must love my children, but how do I balance up the "best" for this one with the "best" for the other, and my wife? I know I should give alms to the poor, but does God want me to give money to this particular person who is likely to spend it on drink? I think I ought to do some work for charity, but what about the time I give my family? This is the area of "discernment of (good or bad) Spirits".

It is an area where there can be doubt about what God wants. And he may not be obliging me under pain of sin. For example: if I do not say my rosary today, I may well feel I am letting God down, but I am under no sort of obligation binding under sin. I would do well to be generous to God and not to ignore his inspiration and I am being less perfectly loving than he would want me to be, but it would be too strict to say that I necessarily sin. Then too, God seems to recommend celibate chastity to all; but it may not be advice that he wants me myself to take. Indeed, since he presumably wants the human race to continue, he presumably cannot be wanting everyone to take it.

1. Three ways God speaks

There seem to be three ways in which God makes his mind known to people, outside the areas of circumstances and obedience. First, he can intervene so forcefully that there can hardly be doubt what he is asking. Our Lady was quite clear that God was communicating with her when the Angel Gabriel appeared to her in Nazareth. St Paul was knocked off his horse and struck blind on the way to Damascus. The message given was unequivocal; he could not pretend he did not know.

A second way is less dramatic, but still very noticeable. We may call it the "mystical" way. Here God intervenes in a way that is exceptional: because there may be no identifiable *cause* that can be identified for its occurrence; because it carries a weight, and probably a sweetness, that is unmistakable. I could not have brought it about by trying to; moreover it points emphatically in the direction God wants. St Joan of Arc may have taken three years to act on what the voices said, but she knew something was happening.

The third way is when God does not come in so forcefully. Perhaps we are not sensitive enough to register the intervention? It is more a matter of his nudging us, winking at us: more like a game of hunt the thimble. You are not told, "The thimble is on top of the TV set". You are told, "warm, warmer, getting hot, not quite so hot, getting cooler . . ." The "warm" and "cold" are known as *Consolation* and *Desolation*.

To find God's will, where circumstances or obedience do not make it clear, the sensible Christian looks at consolation and desolation in the process known

41

as *Discernment of Spirits*. The theory is that the voice of the good spirit, and the wiles of the bad spirit, can be decoded by discerning the movements in one's own spirit.

Is one asked to believe that an angel or a devil might be the reason for the movement; that there are indeed "spirits", in the strict sense, involved in this? Without doubt much of what goes on in my mind and heart is bubbling up from the murky depths of my own psyche, or it might even be dependent on what I had for supper last night. But orthodox Catholics have certainty about the existence of the devil and other bad angels, and about good angels. It is quite certain that the thoughts and feelings and impulses going on inside me speak with the *accents* of the good or bad angels, and that my train of thought slants me towards one or the other. It is perfectly possible that there might be direct influence.

2. Consolation and Desolation

Suppose one is blundering away from God, not necessarily sinfully, maybe unawares. Then of course it is in the interests of the "bad spirit" to keep one going down the slippery slope. One is enticed along by such consolations as the "bad spirit" could contrive: pleasure, self-esteem, career, reputation, ambition – not necessarily always evil, but in this case always more or less inordinate. It will be the work of the "good spirit" to try to pull one up out of this decline or nose-dive. The good spirit therefore cannot help coming in forcefully and painfully. Think for a moment of getting out of bed when one is very tired. Two "voices" come to one; one (very sweet and persuasive) tells one to stay put, the other (rudely intrusive) says "Get up!". Or think of a sexual temptation: two voices, and the good one is exigent and sounds harsh. You see the sort of idea St Ignatius is giving us.

And at this point I drop the quotation marks when I speak of spirit. As has been said, it could well be that there is no metaphor involved in the use of the word. Suppose now one is, perhaps without any merit, groping one's way *towards* God. Here it is in the interests of the good spirit to entice one on ("warm, warmer!"). It is now the bad spirit who is having to twist one off the track. It is he who comes in painfully now.

The enticement of the good spirit is called consolation; the pain of the bad spirit is called desolation.

3. Description

And what exactly are consolation and desolation like? Here is a fair translation of what Ignatius says in various parts of the *Exercises*. Consolation is:

> peace, joy, tranquillity, increase of faith, hope and charity, high spiritual morale, one's hope and reliance on "high" things, tears (sweet tears, that is!).

And Desolation is:

> darkness, doubt, fear, depression, bitterness, remorse, anxiety, low spiritual morale, one's hope in "low" things, muddle and confusion; scrupulosity.

Spend a moment or two identifying what the saint is talking about. Are you in consolation just now, or desolation? What is your predominant state? When did you last experience the other?

The consolation we are considering is *spiritual*. Jesus was in agony in the garden and during the passion and during his death on Calvary. Desolation? At the deepest level, the very deepest, where his will was embracing the Father's, there would have been some sort of peace. If this sounds contrived, consider what would have been in his heart if he had been *failing* to do his Father's will: then there would have been desolation in the fullest sense. No, no matter what the pain and suffering, the martyrs would have told us that it was not just their will, but their joy, to do God's will even in the agony.

Not every pleasure is consolation. A good meal, a hot bath, Beethoven's ninth, all aesthetic experience, is joy; it is not consolation in the sense St Ignatius speaks of. But there is no need to labour the point; a Christian reader is likely to understand what is involved. Read again St Ignatius' description. Desolation is the opposite. A consistent note is that of muddle and confusion. Scrupulosity is the clearest example. Let us readily admit that scrupulosity is usually or always a symptom of a neurosis; but that does not mean that it is not coming with the accents of the enemy. Indeed much of what surfaces as spiritual desolation may have its origins in the murky depths of one's subconscious. And some people, chronic melancholics and depressives, would say that they never have anything except spiritual desolation. That does not mean that they have sinned, or are far from God, or that it is necessarily their fault in any way. It does mean that they have been given a heavy cross to carry – and can be the richer for it. More about the *handling* of desolation later.

Another typical example of desolation springing from muddle and confusion, the stamping ground of the spirit of darkness, is the spiritual squint. The "sacrament" of the present moment as we have seen is one of the great luminous insights in the spiritual life. To see that there is really *only one moment of time*, namely this present moment, is liberating. The past, after all, has gone; nothing I can do can bring it back. The future has not arrived (perhaps, for me, it never will arrive). True, the past may throw a shadow forward, to this present moment: I must pay a debt, say thank you, make an act of contrition. But I cannot enter into that past moment. And the future may throw a shadow backwards to this moment: I must prepare for this exam, write now for the letter to get there on my friend's birthday. But I cannot step into that moment.

Some people spend much of their lives with the spiritual squint – one eye on the past, one eye on the future. And no eye at all on the only real moment that there is – this one. It's like trying to suffer last week's headache today, or next month's toothache. It's to carry too great a burden: the actual burden of life, the cross Jesus lays on me, is not and should not be so unbearable. It is not a burden of eighty years, it is a cross of matchstick size tailor-made for my shoulders: it is the present moment.

But did not our Lord dread the future, and agonize about it in Gethsemane? Are we to be less human than Jesus? No indeed. Our human nature gives us this capacity, which one hopes the animals are spared, of suffering now the anticipated pain of the future. But it is precisely a *present* pain. What is forbidden us is to try to give life, by imagination and by failing to surrender every moment into God's hands, to the factually "unreal" moment. Our Lord, remember, gave us the perfect prayer for the moment of dread: "not my will but thine be done".

4. Handling Consolation and Desolation.

The basic rule, and we must take it for granted that we are in the process of what I have described as "blundering towards God", is so clear, so simple, so obvious, so sweet – and so terrifyingly difficult for most of us: it is that we should always be doing the things that lead to consolation, avoiding the things that lead to desolation.

Is this to say that one must surrender always to the demands of a voracious super-ego, strive to achieve a peace that is ultimately unobtainable? No; if only because, as will be seen later, a fundamental necessity if I am to discern the spirit properly is that I should take advice, particularly in the case of desolation. Nonetheless, it is not impossible that God's will might sometimes, for some, be found in a course of action that seemed less wise or rational and which depended for its plausibility on the insistence of consolation. Is not this often exemplified when one takes a vow of chastity?

A second fundamental principle is obvious when one appreciates that the Blessed Trinity cannot disintegrate through internal strife . . . If the area of obedience belongs to the Word, to our Lord, and the area of discernment belongs to the Holy Spirit, it is impossible that the Holy Spirit should contradict our Lord. The area of discernment, therefore, can never contradict the area of obedience. One feels there is really no such thing, as practised, as loyal dissent. There can only be disobedience, in attitude or in fact.

It may seem harsh to say this, seeing that a number

of Catholic journalists and catechists and theologians, doubtless with the highest motives, achieve popularity and make a good living out of contestation and disobedience. And of course there obviously has to be some sort of discernment (third area) preceding the act of representation (second area). And it is surely clear enough that the Church's history affords fearful examples of the arrogance of power, victorious in part precisely because of the institutionalised subservience that can be a parasitic growth in a Church with divine authority to teach and to govern.

Admit all this, and still the Ignatian and Christian instinct and insight is that the Holy Spirit can only lead me to true obedience.

A third point is important. It was remarked earlier that desolation need not necessarily be the result of sin. It could be, but it needn't be. It may be part of one's personality, permitted by God for a very good reason – namely, to make the muscles of faith grow. Lives of heroic sanctity may be lived in states of desolation. Thérèse of Lisieux had no consolation in her convent; Noël Chabanel was in anguish in the Canadian forests. God produced in them heroism and sanctity of a particular beauty. The trouble is, of course, that one will hardly know if one is being heroic or simply lacking trust and love of God, and there will always be grounds, for the melancholic, to judge he is failing.

5. Rules

i. Perhaps the most important rule is *Go against the advice of the Spirit of Darkness*. It is obvious. Assuming, as we will from now on, that we are aiming towards God, the voice of the good spirit speaks with consolation. Desolation is the mark of the entry or activity of the father of lies. Now who in their senses wants to listen to a liar? In desolation, the message, the accents, the style are all those of the enemy. Of Christ's enemy too: of the one who rejoiced in the Crucifixion. To listen to that voice is the beginnings of treason; it is certainly to allow oneself to enter an occasion of the sin of failing to trust God.

In desolation, therefore, one does the exact opposite of what the desolation says. One tries not to listen, and one's action is to aim in the precisely opposite direction. After all, if the father of *lies* says "Go left", then the good Spirit (whom I can't hear) must be saying "Go right". For example, one is praying, let us say in total aridity, and if the voice is saying "Pack it in; you're useless at this; you're insulting God by pretending that what you're doing is prayer; leave it, and do something that is useful and is not a complete waste of time", then it is obvious from the very tone and accents that it is not the voice of Jesus. Whose is it? The voice of my psyche doubtless, but chiming in surely with the voice of the spirit of darkness. Therefore the right response is precisely to stay praying for a bit longer, precisely what the enemy and the liar is trying to stop you doing. For Jesus, inaudible though he be, must be saying the opposite: "Thank you for your prayer; what you are doing is precious to me; I appreciate your good desires; you long for union with me – trust me, I give it".

Here of course is the only rational way of overcoming the neurotic symptom of scrupulosity. An insistent and torturing voice is telling me to do such and such (to worry about the past, to go over a previous confession, to be obsessive about protecting other people from germs . . .). The voice of the Good Spirit? No! Blasphemy to think so: he could not speak like that. So . . . the voice of the enemy? Well, I suppose it must be.

Will I listen to the one who crucified Jesus? Will I take his advice? Will I step into treason?

But if I do not follow this voice I may risk damnation!

Yes, *if* the voice is trustworthy. But if not, to reduce the dilemma to its absurd basis, then in order to avoid the impossibly remote chance of falling into mortal sin, as the liar is insistent will happen, I will *certainly* be putting myself into the occasion of committing the venial sin of lack of trust of God.

I spell this out, not because in the modern Church one comes across scrupulosity much (for good or evil the obsession behind it takes different forms; perhaps the presence of sin and the fear of hell seem more remote than in previous generations) but because in the case of St Ignatius himself it would seem likely that this, under the action of grace, was the way he fought through to freedom from scruples.

ii. A principle of action allied to this can be very useful. It is, *never change a previous good decision in a time of desolation*. The reason is clear. Here I am, led in a time perhaps of sweetness and consolation, under the influence of grace, to make a good decision. Now comes darkness. Isn't it obvious that this is the worst possible time to change direction? When the voice telling me to change is that of the liar, good sense dictates I should go on as before. If the captain of a ship at sea loses sight of land through fog, if the radar breaks down, and the inertial navigation system – surely that is the worst possible moment to change course and speed from what he knew was right before?

iii. Another good rule is to talk about the desolations to someone who could help. Sometimes almost anyone might be capable of identifying that what was befogging one was muddle, confusion, nonsense. But, always provided they were orthodox and sensible and devout, normally one's confessor or superior could be the person.

iv. We must expect desolation, and we must expect it to come through the shape of our own personality. If you are a mean, melancholy, introverted type you must expect the spirit of darkness to speak with conforming accents. If you are a self-satisfied and crashing extravert, you must expect another approach. Hamlet wasn't tempted the same way Falstaff was.

6. A subtlety

Nothing much has been said directly about behaviour in consolation. Partly that is because it is fairly obvious; one goes on doing the things that bring it. But there is one point that is important.

There is an instance when, correctly progressing towards God, being rewarded and enticed by consolation, being aware of desolation as a warning that one may be running off the line, there can be a sweetness and a consolation that is to be mistrusted. St Ignatius speaks of it as "the spirit of darkness disguised as the angel of light".

Realise that there is a supposition that is very important. I have spoken about "blundering one's way to God" perhaps through no particular merit of one's own. Suppose a person is really trying very hard to do God's will and, always excepting weakness and slackness and cowardice, it is true to say that there really is nothing of deliberate malice in his life, and that he is free of any embraced slavery. Deliberate and contrived venial sin is absent. Then it is clear enough that the spirit of darkness is unlikely to succeed in getting the person to step out of God's will through sin. Any ordinary temptation would be so obvious that the man would not be likely to fall for it. Any successful temptation, if not to sin, at least to something that is less to God's glory, will have to be to *something good*.

And it will come accompanied by consolation. How to detect "the serpent's tail"? Probably experience.

An obvious example might be of someone who, lazy by nature, is drawn to undertake some work to the glory of God, which incidentally involves a good deal of uncongenial labour. He is aware that he has in the past shirked duty through laziness; he sees that the work is good; he certainly could do it if he really exerted himself . . . and he takes on more than he can handle. The result is failure in God's work. Or a beggar solicits money; the passer-by knows he is by nature selfish; he fears being uncharitable and giving in to his weakness. He can see the man is likely to be an alcoholic – but he gives. The act, notice, was "good" in itself. It *is* a good thing to give to the poor, normally. It is a good thing to be generous with time and effort for God; it is a good thing to exert oneself against one's predominant fault; there was a genuine drawing of sweetness . . . and God's will was not done.

How does experience teach? One would learn by the

51

bad effects later, of course. But in some cases the very flavour of the attraction, sometimes with an element of *compulsion* to the good can be a sign.

7. Should I contrive to experience consolation and desolation?

Consolation and desolation can guide me. If I am aiming towards God then normally as has been said at length, consolation indicates the way I should go, and desolation should deter me from wandering off. Therefore I am not being ridiculous if, at least from time to time, I make some sort of note (perhaps copying out bits of scripture that speak to me, perhaps very briefly pinning down how I feel, if there is a "spiritual" element in it) to keep track of what is going on in my spirit.

Just as a cloud chamber shows the track of an electron, so movements in my spirit may show the track of God's finger (or a trace of Satan). And to know either can be useful.

It is worth noting the obvious, that there is no sense in trying to provoke desolation. Who would want to? And most of us get enough of it anyway. To speak madly, if I want real certainty of real desolation what I need to do is glaringly obvious. Let me just commit one deliberate venial sin; let me knowingly disregard God's will in any tiniest aspect. That, for sure, will bring movement in my spirit. As St John of the Cross says, a tiny thread will be enough to tie a bird down. Desolation is at my behest any time I care to sin.

If, however, to experience consolation and desolation can be useful to help me find God's will, then it would be reasonable from time to time to set up, as it were, laboratory conditions in which to detect them. The best way of doing this is to be alone, in silence, and to pray a lot, for some days. Then the movements are likely to become magnified. The best structure for this is a retreat of a special sort. In addition, there may be a "director" who, being outside oneself, may be able to throw light. The prayer, it should be said, should not be about oneself and one's spiritual life . . . it should be real prayer, to and "about" God. You see the sunlight not by looking at the sun.

It is the Spiritual Exercises of St Ignatius which is probably the best sort of retreat, and the best instrument in the Church, for this. Ideally, they would be made for about thirty days, with silence and with four or five periods of about an hour's prayer during the day (and night), with frequent access to the director. This is hard. It is not something God would want everyone to do, and the ones he would not want to do it could be much holier and more "advanced" than those he does. In passing, the obvious point may be made that the expense of something like this would make it a rare and extraordinary luxury for most people. Only Religious normally can do things like this . . .

Commonly, a reasonable effort towards a condensed version of the Exercises could be made in eight or even six days, perhaps with conferences being given to a group. Or the Exercises could be given over a period of months to someone who is living life at home as normal, but seeing a director from time to time, and praying for perhaps an hour each day.

Since consolation, for our purposes, can be taken to be the sign of the guidance of the Holy Spirit, it goes without saying that one should always "strive" for this, in the sense that one always tries to avoid anything against his will and to do everything that is in line with it. In practice then the simple daily, monthly, yearly fidelity to prayer and the sacraments is essential.

8. Direction?

The serious Christian would do well to acquire some experience of the movements of the spirit, and to be aware that very often "feelings" are to be disregarded and that one "goes by faith". And yet God has used, and can still use, our spiritual feelings to guide us. Someone to talk things out with occasionally can be useful, even though such people can be hard to find.

The ideal director would be someone with a lot of common sense, and with feet firmly on the ground, and close to God. Courses are run nowadays on discernment, but wise men would say that the acquisition of a few rules of thumb would be all that could be expected.

For many people it would be fair to say that "direction" is not really urgent. There need be no reason for God to be saying anything but what is very obvious. But even in such a case, it could be useful, perhaps at lengthy intervals, to say out loud what is going on inside one.

One obvious criterion for direction: never go to anyone who is in disobedience to the Pope and the Church. If the person can't obey in the "second area", there is little hope that their judgement in the "third area" is going to be reliable.

9. Making a decision

In order to make a decision one uses reason first. Unless God is going to intervene in the two more or less dramatic ways mentioned in Chapter 4 section 2, one has to think. And even after those two, one is not absolved from being intelligent.

One obviously is not going to decide for anything sinful. One prays about the courses of action that lie open, and notes the movement of consolation and desolation.

If the decision is not a once-and-for-all one, as: Shall I marry? Shall I go into religious life? Shall I take out this mortgage? Shall I buy this car? then a good plan is to *experiment*. "Lord, I don't know whether it is this, or this, or this, that you want. For the time being I am going to try *this*, and see if this is the one".

And how would one know if it is what he wants? Because if it is, he will "reward" with consolation ("warm!"). If it isn't, then in all likelihood there will be desolation.

What should I give in the way of alms? Let me experiment, and see what brings consolation. How much should I pray? How should I pray? Where should I pray? Should I pray with others? How should I do penance? How much should I fast? How much time should I give to such and such activity? I don't know. I can see a lot of reasonable positions to take up. So I will experiment by doing *this* for three months, or six, and see what God says about it.

Of course God may have given a pretty clear indication already, in what is perhaps the "second area". There is no need to "decide" whether frequent confession of venial sin is a good thing; the Church encourages it. Nor whether adoration of the Blessed Sacrament is desirable. Nor if contraception is objectively wrong, and homosexual acts. Nor if one should campaign for women priests.

Perhaps the most important thing in making a decision is this: that I should be absolutely determined that I really do want what God wants. If he sees I would be ready to cut off my right hand to know what he wants, then I could be reasonably sure that he could make his will known to me. But if in fact my life proves that I am ducking his known will fairly regularly, and have areas which I would not open up for discussion with God: if in other words I am not free to want to know his will, then I can save my breath in asking him.

St Ignatius has a word for the right attitude: Detachment. It does not mean detachment in feeling, it means that my *will* is able to be in equipoise, ready to embrace whatever he indicates, no matter what the cost.

For this, St Ignatius encourages us to ask to be chosen by God to what is most repugnant . . . if I really am that determined to be free of enchainments, even to what is innocent, even to the extent of asking for what has most of the Cross – simply because it *has* his Cross in it – then there is every chance that God could make his mind known to me. This is hard doctrine. So is his advice that if one wants a grace, in this case to know God's will, one must of course pray; but in addition, he says, it helps to add weight to prayer of petition to do a bit of penance.

Part II

Ways of knowing

God exists
Determinism fails;
Spirit exists
Right and wrong

God exists

1. The classical argument from contingency

We all know that everything that we come across is linked to, and in some way depends on, everything else. You and I are linked to the air we breathe. We are linked to the sun – even to all the galaxies in the sky. If we cannot see them there still must be some effect from their gravity. Ultimately we must be linked to every atom and molecule that there is and ever has been: nature is an unimaginably vast and complex unity. Put it another way: everything that there is depends on other things for being the precise way it is, or even for its very existence.

The technical and shorthand way of expressing this fact is to say that everything we meet in nature is *contingent* – depends on other things. Now if that is so, nothing we meet in nature can give a complete and adequate explanation of itself, or of anything else. For instance: there is a rail-card lying on my untidy desk at this moment. To explain why it is there I have to explain the existence of railways, the existence of trees (my desk is made of wood), my existence. I would have to go back to the beginning of the universe, the "Big Bang" if there was a Big Bang, in order adequately and completely to explain the rail-card on my desk.

For anything that exists there must be a reason sufficient for its existence. I might not understand how a thing exists, but I have to see that there are circumstances or events that could (somehow) provide for its existence.

The reader I have in mind would probably agree with this statement. But it is a fact that many people would not, for it seems to be asking "why" in a place where they say there is no place for a why. And yet all science progresses by asking why, and to flinch from asking is to deny the possibility of progress. Therefore it seems reasonable to demand that the first fact of science, the fact of the Big Bang, should demand scrutiny for its having happened. If this position is denied, then the argumentation that follows would indeed be irrelevant. But to claim that the asking why is to be forbidden in this one instance needs justification which most of us could never produce.

Some would say the Big Bang *is* the reason. But the Big Bang itself demands a reason; I do not have to be able to show how it happened, but I must admit that there would have to be a reason for it happening, circumstances that enabled it to take place. But obviously if there ever was *nothing,* not one atom, not one pulse of energy, then plainly there never could be anything. But things exist! Therefore there must have been *something* to start the Big Bang.

Suppose that there was an eternally existing universe? Let us say that the Big Bang resulted from the collapse of some preceding system, and let us imagine that collapse and bang was a process that had happened for all eternity. (I say, let's *imagine;* is it possible actually to *conceive* this?) Would there now be an adequate explanation for my rail-card being on the desk? Surely it simply *has* to be there, seeing that the universe is as it is? If I could see in all its ramifications the history of every atom and molecule that has ever existed, there could be no possibility of the rail-card being anywhere else. The very existence of an eternally existing universe surely would be sufficient reason for everything being as it is?

No. There is still the need for an explanation of why the whole complex exists – and so far I am baulked of a proper answer. Just because the universe had always existed, the mind would still crave a reason as to how or why it all got there. Imagine a locomotive and series of trucks linked together on a circular track perfectly fitted to hold them. The movement of each depends on the movement of the next; and on the rails on which they run. But that has not given a final explanation – you still have to explain how the whole set-up got there in the first place.

Either explanation, Big Bang and sudden start, or an eternally existent universe, demands a sufficient reason for happening, a reason that satisfies the mind. But it is obvious that no contingent thing can possibly provide the reason, for the contingent thing looks outside itself for the reason for its being the way it is.

Therefore the reason must be *non-contingent;* that is, it must be something that depends not on other things for its existence but on itself. Something therefore that does not need any other reason for being, but is its own reason; something that could not *not-be.* This is what we call God.

If this, "God", started the universe or at least holds an eternally existing universe in being, it must have intelligence - for intelligence exists, and it cannot be less than what it produces. And what an intelligence it must have! But with intelligence, it must be a person: *he,* let us say, not it. And it must have will (what will!) to make the decision to start it all, or to hold it all.

If you have never really believed much in God, or postponed thinking about him, or felt that there were so many contradictory and ridiculous religions around that the whole thing wasn't worth thinking about, I hope things start to get a bit scary for you . . . You see I think you have proved that a personal God exists; and persons have to be responded to; and this person is in charge of the whole universe – and of you.

There are immediate objections. The universe looks, the bit of it we can see, often a very horrible place in parts. If God is responsible, we can be excused for thinking as little as possible about him. But that is to move too fast. First things first: his existence has to be registered before we think about what he is like. "The problem of evil" is a real objection, but it is not the first fact about God. So far all we have got to is that God exists, he knows and wills, he is unimaginable, he is responsible for everything that happens.

The ideal would be to go out tonight to the top of a hill, in the silence and the cold and the dew, and look at the stars. But the reader I have in mind would, typically, be living in a northern housing estate: the sky will be overcast, there aren't any accessible lonely hills, there aren't any stars visible because of cloud cover – and even if there were, the light-pollution of our cities would make them invisible. So do the next best thing. Why not go to your room, assuming you have it to yourself, sit down and put your head in your hands and say to this person "If you exist, help me". Help me what? "Help me know you. You hold the universe in existence, you have will, you know me, you see me as clearly as you see the furthest galaxy 14 billion light years away (and light travels at 186,000 miles a second), a galaxy which is perhaps only a billion years away from the Big Bang . . . You see, hold in existence, every atom and molecule and every pulse of energy in the universe . . . Help me know you, meet you".

Don't try to imagine; don't try to work up a feeling (perhaps a feeling will come, perhaps the basic religious experience of awe; but don't work to get it). Just think quietly, be still, be honest, and perhaps in time with your breathing gently keep on saying "Help me".

Don't try to picture an old man with a beard on a throne, don't even try to imagine white light, or weight, or silence. Just admit the presence of God ("present" because he is acting, willing you to exist) and submit to him as fact.

2. Some attributes of God

We can work out from reason a good deal of what God must be like. We can see first that he exists, and that if he knows and wills he is a person. There is a big difficulty here. The fact is that if we wanted to be really accurate, we could hardly use words about God at all. The most basic word I suppose is "*is*". But God doesn't exist, doesn't do his "*is*-ing" the way anything else does. Everything else *is* because something else *is;* but God is not like that – he is not contingent, he is necessary; his being is different from the being of every other thing there is or ever has been. There isn't a word for his sort of existing. That is because we can really only use words properly about what comes within the range of our experience or about what we can clearly conceive. It is not that God is something so vague we can't speak properly about him, on the contrary he is too real and too solid.

And so we ought really to switch into a special sort of mental mode when we talk about God, and realise that whatever we say is more UNlike what we mean than it is like. For instance, about God being a person. The first danger is that we should do our *thinking* with our imagination. It is hard to think of "person" without having some vague picture of someone with arms and legs. Now that is not the essence of a person, it is something to do with the human beings we have met: we have to learn to reason, to make *concepts* without being deflected by the imagination.

There is more we can find out about necessary being, about God, from reason. He is not dependent on anything, as we have seen. That means there can be no "before" or "after" with God. If there were a "before", his existence now would be consequent and dependent on it; if there were an "after", it would be the consequence of what is now. So God is completely outside time. He has all his being at one moment . . . *Now!* Nor can there be any matter in God, because one bit of matter is dependent on other bits, and there is no dependence in necessary being. Nor can there be space in God, because what has no parts or bits has no space. And something in space is dependent again – on the spread of its parts through the space.

Therefore God is changeless, for if a thing has no parts and does not exist in time, there can be no change. One can think of time as the measurement of change, and where there is no matter and no time there is no change. This leads us to what may seem the most fundamental thing about God: He is infinite. He produced a universe by his will, and from nothing. After all, if he fashioned it from some pre-existent thing, we have to explain where that came from; if we want to think of an endless chain – and we have been through this before - we only postpone, or rather sidetrack, our arrival at necessary being. The distance from NO THING to anything, even a single molecule, is infinite – there is no connection. God's power is infinite. It's not just that to hold the enormous universe in existence demands a lot of power, the point is that to create anything, to be the sufficient reason for anything to exist, demands infinite power.

One final point. God is single, unique. There cannot be two Gods. Why not? After all, it would be convenient to think as some have in past history that a good God made all the nice and pleasant things, and a bad God made evil things and was responsible for suffering. And one could make a case for the conflict we each feel in ourselves between good and evil being the working out of a battle between these two principles. But it won't do. We have seen that nothing can exist save from the action of "necessary being", the one thing that cannot not exist. There cannot be two such beings: either they are influenced by each other and so are "dependent" on each other – which means that they are not self-existent; or one of them is totally irrelevant to the other, and unknown – in other words does not exist.

All this is to use reason. It tells us true things about God, but it is limited because reason can never plumb God. Endlessly more important is what God has told us through Revelation about himself. And the picture we get there is very different. The Bible tells us of a God who changes his mind, who is angry, who can be

65

placated. Granted all occasions when we take reasonable liberties to translate biblical imagery into our own categories, to make it intelligible, it is still difficult to think of the "God of reason" as not being a misleading idol compared to the one true God, the father of Abraham Isaac and Jacob, and the father of our Lord. There are mysteries not only in God but in human intellect which are impenetrable. We have to expect that. The candle-flame to lead us deeper into reasoning about God is known as *analogy,* about which these few pages are silent.

If you want to accept all this you have come a long way. You would be ready to hold that God does not only exist, but that he is a person – he has knowledge and will. He is "outside" space and time. He has no before and after; he has all his existence at every moment of out time. He is infinite: infinitely wise, infinitely powerful. Nothing in the whole universe exists without his knowledge and his will. That includes you and me.

Determinism fails;
Spirit exists

1. Materialism and determinist theories have a fatal flaw

Much of what follows in this section is guided by C.S.Lewis' *Miracles*.

We are all agreed that our thinking takes place in our brain cells, and involves electrical charges and chemical changes and alterations in synapses. But of course such things are part of the material world, and all of them are dependent on the ordinary workings of matter, and on the behaviour of atoms and molecules and electrical charges and pulses of energy and all the complex of activity that science investigates and can measure. And the changes come about through the ordinary workings of matter: the situation in the universe at this moment of time must be dependent on, and explicable by, the state of the universe in the fraction of a nano-second before. It surely cannot be dependent on anything else?

But the state of the universe in that precise moment was dependent on its state before that . . . and so on indefinitely back. In fact, everything that happens (that is, the condition of every atom and molecule and pulse of energy in the universe) cannot be in any way different from the way it actually is. What is, is *determined;* cannot be otherwise. This must be the case if all there is in the universe is atoms and molecules and electrical charges, if in fact the "materialist" position (which says that nothing exists except matter) is true.

If everything is indeed determined by the workings of atoms and molecules, that position described must be true. But there are other materialist positions. A Marxist might say that everything that happened in history was determined by the economic situation. Some Freudians might say that everything man did was determined by the conflict of his unconscious desires with his conditioning.

Perhaps you can see the difficulty in their positions? Do they mean EVERYTHING is determined? If they do, it would mean that they think that all thought (which after all depends on the actions of atoms and molecules in our brains) is also determined: but that means that I cannot be thinking anything except what I am thinking; and that means that I cannot be claiming *truth* for what I say – every single thing that happens in my brain, even my feeling that this statement is true, is determined and cannot be other than it is. It would mean that the materialist scientist, or Marxist, or Freudian cannot *not* be saying and thinking what he is saying. And if he can't help thinking and saying it, how can he claim that he is right in thinking it is true?

You see, the determinist can certainly feel convinced by something, he can feel sure that such and such a fact is true. But the very *feeling* of certainty and conviction can only be through the predetermined action of atoms and molecules. His feeling of certainty can have no validity, for what makes one come to truth is valid inference by reasoning. This would certainly demand the working of atoms and molecules in the brain, but if it depended on them and nothing else as *cause,* it would be the helpless predetermined result of the situation among those atoms a split second before. Examples given by C.S.Lewis are useful: "You would say that because you are a man" – implying the statement is invalid because caused by circumstances; and "The whole is equal to the sum of its parts" – a truth seen, not just an expectation verified.

So imagine the case of the materialist. He says to himself: "At last! I have proved, from my scientific studies, that nothing exists except matter. That means I have proved that God does not exist!" But if nothing exists except matter, then everything, including the working of his brain cells, including his conviction that he has proved something, is as inevitable as a hiccup and no more intelligent. He has proved, if you like, that proofs are impossible; he has reasoned to the impossibility of reasoning. If he's right – he's wrong.

And it's not just his reasoning that he has disproved. He feels as we all do a duty to proclaim the truth. "I *must* explain to others that belief in God is a fallacy". But his sense of obligation is a delusion too – he cannot help feeling that. No blame, no praise, can ever pass his lips – everything that everyone else may ever do or say is meaningless and can merit no sanction.

Well this sort of universe is impossible to live in. So the argument must be wrong. But the steps in it were logical enough. Look at it again. It must therefore be the presupposition that was wrong, namely that all that existed was atoms and molecules and electrical charges. So, there must be something other than atoms and molecules and electrical charges that exist: there *must* be, if I am ever going to be able to reason properly, if I am going to have a right to praise or blame. There is a technical term for this "thing"; we call it *Spirit*.

Why do not more people see the point of this argument and accept that materialism and determinism are self-contradictory? Probably because, even the wisest, they have never heard it. Possibly too because they hope that natural selection would provide the means whereby the automatic working of matter, the predetermined by-laws of chemistry and energy, could give the power to *reason*.

Here is C.S.Lewis in *Miracles,* Chapter 3, The Cardinal Difficulty of Naturalism: "natural selection could operate only by eliminating responses that were biologically hurtful and multiplying those which tended to survival. But it is not conceivable that any improvement of responses could ever turn them into acts of insight, or even remotely tend to do so. The relation between response and stimulus is utterly different from that between knowledge and the truth known . . . knowledge is achieved by experiments and inference from them, not by refinement of the response".

In all this it is very important to distinguish between what one imagines and what one can conceive, between an image and a concept. The word spirit makes me think of something vague and spooky, pale and drifty and formless and thin; or, it makes me think of courage and exuberance ("Keep your spirits up"); or of something "inside" or motivating (the spirit of Nazi Germany, or of the 1960s, or of "team spirit"). We must try to get rid of these images when we want to reason and think – as opposed to imagine. Better to think of it as you "think" of electricity or gravity – pretty much imageless. But one cannot not have images when one thinks; the one I try to have is of light focused at a point, and sort of humming and zinging with energy . . . and, a useful fancy of C.S.Lewis, as in some way *heavier* than matter.

And we, evidently, are spirit as well as matter. There is no doubt that we are made up of matter. But there can be no doubt either that we have "powers" somehow over and above matter. This something, spirit, is obviously active and can dictate to matter. It is in some sense "superior" for that reason. It may be that the relationship of spirit to thought is more or less one of *cause,* and that matter, my brain, is the *condition.*

The distinction is very simple. The *cause* of the radio programme is what is going on in the studio and through the radio waves, but the entirely necessary condition for hearing it is a radio set. Throw a brick at the radio and you cannot hear the programme; put a bullet through my brain and you stop me thinking. It doesn't follow that my brain is making my thoughts.

How would one have to respond to this, if the thought is new? "Lord, there is more to me than I thought. And you and I have something in common. My thinking, my judgement of right and wrong, has some sort of relation to yours, and is the most important thing about me. It is my feelings, Lord that seem so important to me – but I may share them with the animals; help me to see that it is my judgements and my decisions which are spiritual and which relate me to you".

2. Spirit is immortal

All living things seem to die. This is because they are made up of matter, and matter changes, and some of the changes result in their life-principle – what one can reasonably call "soul", even if it is that of a vegetable – no longer being able to continue. They die, in short. But what has no parts presumably cannot change in the same sort of way. No parts, no matter, no chemical changes, no conducting of electricity . . . presumably no death.

The soul in man is, we say, spiritual. It is in the life principle that the spiritual element operates in conjunction with the matter. In which case one would have to say that the soul is immortal. Its continued existence after the death of the body it informed is conceivable. Presumably nothing of feeling, what was dependent on nerves, of desire in the ordinary sense, of pity as such, would endure: only those exercises of will and intellect which essentially belonged to spirit. Choice, and the determinations it had effected would remain. This is the philosophical basis for thought on heaven and hell.

Of course Christians believe that human soul is not meant to endure in this truncated way, and that there will be a triumphant, or catastrophic, rejoining somehow of soul to the "body". What this means is also impossible to imagine, but could do with careful and reasoned thought. This may help. My body can be described as matter and energy for which my spirit has some sort of aptitude and relationship: I do not have to picture arms and legs, but I can rejoice to know that the effects of physical experiences – which I shared with animals – and the resultant emotions which were dignified by my human possession – and which were to the glory of God and which affected my spirit, will still be present. Not just the consequences of spiritual actions, my choices, but the experience of joy, pleasure, effective pity; the experience of beauty, tenderness – all these will be mine for all eternity, but immeasurably intensified. The lowliest good things will be eternal as well as the highest.

3. Another argument for immortality

This line of thought is clear and can be stated very shortly. I do not think it is likely to convince anyone who does not already accept the immortality of the soul; but for those who do, it adds weight.

One can take as a principle that nature does nothing in vain. For instance, if nature provides acorns, there is bound to be a chance of an oak tree resulting. If animals feel hunger, it is because they need food; therefore there must be such a thing as food. Of course people starve, and of course if I scatter acorns at the North Pole no tree will grow. But the fact remains, there cannot be anything in nature, including natural appetite, which does not point to the possibility of fulfilment under favourable conditions.

Not of course that there is not "waste" in nature. All those lemmings pouring over the cliff . . . all the sperm wasted in conception . . . is not this an example of nature doing things in vain? No; the fittest sperm makes the ovum; the unnecessary lemmings kill themselves. Even if only one sperm survived, only one lemming, the loss of the rest is for some sort of purpose.

Human beings all desire happiness. If you meet someone who enjoys being miserable it simply means that he gets his satisfaction and fulfilment – which is what is really meant by happiness – in a peculiar way. We do not just want pleasure, but contentment and deep and permanent satisfaction of our most profound needs. We long for our hunger for love and beauty to be permanently satisfied.

Satisfaction of this sort, however, is completely outside our experience. We have never come across anybody who has had it. And yet we long for it. This satisfaction is plainly not obtainable in this life: even if we had what seems to be a perfection of bliss of every sort, one vital element would be lacking: this happiness is threatened, it will not last and we know it will not last. But what we can conceive, unexperienced though it is, is total and unthreatened fulfilment.

But nature does nothing in vain . . . this sort of joy must therefore be obtainable. If it is not obtainable in this life, there must be another where it is.

And the response to this? Surely: "My Lord and my God, it is you I long for, you I love above all. Guide me to yourself".

Right and wrong

The few lines which follow are obviously too short and too inadequate to pretend to be even an outline of traditional ethics. Their purpose is to provide a few notions and some vocabulary for young people who may be quite uninstructed, but which, if developed by a teacher, could be useful.

1. Goodness, virtue, vice

When we talk of a good footballer, we mean one who is good at getting goals. Even if he beats his wife he is still a good footballer. A good liar is a villain, but one who is convincing in his *metier* of being a fraud. *Good* therefore has a notion of efficiency about it. And when we speak of a good man, we mean a man who is efficient at the business of being human.

What the *good* man has done is to work on his nature, on what he is, so that he has made a success of himself. This working on his nature modifies it, improves it. It is done by modifying it, fitting it with what one could call a sort of *second nature*.

That is what we mean by *virtue:* it is a sort of second nature, a *habit* built up – often with great difficulty by repeated acts often in the teeth of opposing enticements and perhaps over years – which makes it comparatively easy to be good. And *vice* is the opposite. An interesting thing for the Christian to note is that to do a good thing through habit is more admirable, and more meritorious in God's eyes, than when there has to be a great effort in it.

2. What makes an action good?

It has to be an action that makes us an "efficient" human being. That means an action that will efficiently lead us to fulfilment. But our real fulfilment is in eternity, so it will not necessarily involve the satisfaction of a present need.

One can see that in any action or intention there are three things:

Motive, "end". If this is bad, obviously every-thing else is vitiated. For instance, to give to a needy person is in itself good, but if my giving is a bribe to him to do something evil, then my gift is wrong.

Circumstances. These might not make an action good or bad, but they might increase the goodness or badness. It's bad to hit an old lady; but if she is my grandmother, it's even worse.

Means, "object". This is the thing done, normally the visible part of the procedure.

For an action to be good, all three elements have to be good, or at least, in the case of circumstances, not bad. For the action to be bad, any one only needs to be bad. This is not an arbitrary rule. It is easy enough to see it is so in the case of evil. As regards goodness it may not be so clear. What we mean by goodness is, as has been stated, that there should be a sort of "efficiency", that the thing has the property of being fully itself. Well, any single defect will destroy this. He is not a good man if he beats his wife; he is not a good footballer if he shoots wide; it is not a good action if the act itself, or the motive, or the circumstances are evil.

3. End and means

There is an old saying of traditional morality, "The end does not justify the means". That is to say that a good motive does not make a bad act justifiable. To finish the second World War was a good end; to drop the atom bomb was, most would say, an evil means. Even if it saved the lives of thousands of people, including Japanese lives which would have been lost if the war had continued, it was – say many – a bad means. So, too, to get information from a suspected bomb-planter is a good end; to torture him would be a bad means.

4. The principle of double effect

Distinguish what has been said from what follows now. Every action you or I could do might be good, but it also has many other effects, some of which may be bad. For instance, the fact that you are reading this page means that you cannot at the same time be writing a letter, saying prayers, watching television, talking to your grandmother. You could say that I am responsible for your being unable to do any of these good things: at least certainly it is true that *you* are responsible. Does that mean that you should not be reading this? No. What you want, what you intend, is to do a good thing, and you can tolerate the regrettable side-effects which are inevitable. The rule is that I am entitled to do a good action even if I perceive there may be evil effects, provided I do not will these evil effects directly, and that the bad effects do not "outweigh" the good.

In war the traditional moral view is that for a good

end – the destruction of this strong-point, say – I am entitled to use weapons even though I foresee that there may be death to innocent civilians. It would of course be wrong to use the killing of civilians to achieve my "good" end: hence terror bombing, and all terrorism, is wrong.

5. Things "intrinsically immoral"?

The traditional view, and that authoritatively taught by the ordinary magisterium of the Church, is that there are some things the doing of which will always be wrong, and that no excuse would ever allow. That is the Church's position, but at the time of writing it is easy to find the contrary view taught in many so-called Catholic colleges, seminaries and universities.

Could it ever be right to commit incest or paedophilia? Most would say that these actions would always be evil. Those who take positions known as "situation ethics" or "proportionalism" would, I think, argue that you have to do a sort of moral calculation and weigh up whether greater good might result – rather as one might in evaluating a case of "double effect".

The orthodox Catholic position is that no calculation of effects is valid, because a *moral* evil outweighs, is in a different order from, all other possible consequences.

Conclusion

These few lines are meant to open ideas to people who have never thought of them, not to answer problems, and they are inadequate for a proper study. But they are inadequate for a more serious reason. In Part II the name of Christ has not been mentioned, and yet it is *He* who is "The Way, the Truth and the Life", and to neglect Him is to wander off course, to blunder and to starve. So why the neglect? Because for the readers I envisage in these chapters, the assault to their faith, in college or university and across the coffee table, is not likely often to come from theological difficulties but from philosophical ones – usually pretty stupid ones. The answers have to be, for most hearers, on philosophical lines.

Bibliography

The following books will be helpful for further reading or reference:

Abandonment to Divine Providence, J P de Caussade

The Belief of Catholics, Ronald Knox

The Catechism of the Catholic Church

An Introduction to Catholic Social Teaching,
    Rodger Charles, SJ

Introduction to Christianity, Cardinal Joseph Ratzinger
    (Pope Benedict XVI)

Map of Life, Frank Sheed

Mere Christianity, C S Lewis

Miracles, C S Lewis

Sacrament of the Present Moment, J P de Caussade

The Spiritual Exercises of St Ignatius of Loyola

Theology and Sanity, Frank Sheed

Theology for Beginners, Frank Sheed

www.ingramcontent.com/pod-product-compliance
Lightning Source LLC
Chambersburg PA
CBHW071836020426
42331CB00007B/1751